Strangers

A play

Colin and Mary Crowther

Samuel French—London
www.samuelfrench-london.co.uk

FOR AMATEUR PRODUCTION ENQUIRIES

UNITED KINGDOM AND WORLD
EXCLUDING NORTH AMERICA
plays@samuelfrench.co.uk
020 7255 4302/01

Each title is subject to availability from Samuel French,
depending upon country of performance.

CHARACTERS

Riverwoman 60, distracted, but resolute
Fisherman 40 plus, observant, imperturbable
Stranger 40, volatile, but vulnerable
Girl (voice only) 8, apprehensive

SCENE

An abandoned jetty at the water's edge

Time — the present

PRODUCTION NOTES

Whether you opt for a realistic or stylized approach, this play offers you the chance to create a really stunning setting very easily — just a platform and a ramp — so try to make the platform as big as possible. Fifteen feet by five or six would be ideal. The ramp is on the point of collapse at one point but that effect is created by good acting and sound effects not by complicated and potentially dangerous mechanics. It is the Stranger's reaction — falling then scrabbling backwards up it — that makes us believe in what is happening.

Set

Do try to use the punt idea. It will look amazing and is so easy to achieve — a punt, after all, is only a rectangular shape and how you get it to move will provide any good Stage Manager with lots of fun. The Fisherman could move on to the jetty and occupy the fishing seat at some point or simply remain where he is, in which case no fishing seat is required. Whichever you choose you will need a 3-piece rod for coarse fishing set up with its line stretched out into the water DRC and we suggest you remove the hook to avoid it snagging on lights or drapes.

Effects

Strands of mist cling to the base of the reeds and the ramp as the curtain rises, but please note: strands of mist *not* blanket fog! This effect can be repeated at the end, when the Fisherman steps down on to the water, but try it out in rehearsal first, because it can be noisy and draw attention to itself, which would not be desirable. If it can come from behind the reeds at the place where he steps on to the water, all the better.

Costume

Riverwoman: she wears old clothes in earthy, sun-faded colours: a plain three-quarter length cardigan over a shapeless T- shirt and a long gathered skirt, the bottom of which is wet from her trek across the meadow.
Fisherman: he wears faded blue dungarees, bleached by sun and sea and daubed with streaks of grey and green: appropriately, the colours of water.

Stranger: she wears a jacket over black jeans and jumper, but something about her — jacket or scarf perhaps is in fiery autumn colours. Her hair is swept back severely.

We have deliberately reduced the moves in the text to a minimum to give you scope to develop your own.

We suggest that the play is more effective if the child does not appear but speaks her lines – live – from the wings.

Finally, though the play is set in the Fens, this should not be interpreted as requiring a Norfolk burr. The Fens is simply a metaphor for the isolation of the characters, so no attempt at a local accent need be attempted.

Enjoy!

Other plays by Colin and Mary Crowther
published by Samuel French Ltd

Calling
Just Passing
Noah's Ark
Reflections
Silent Night
Till We Meet Again
An Untimely Frost (formerly The Lost Garden)

Plays by Colin Crowther
published by Samuel French Ltd

Footprints in the Sand
Tryst

STRANGERS

An old wooden jetty by the water's edge, a dangerous, shifting boundary between land and sea, a place to set out from, not a place to linger. Even the birds sound lonely here, their calls shrieking and booming across the still water

UL *leads, over marsh, to dry land. The river, now largely stagnant, once flowed from* DL *past* URC *to off* R. *Centre stage, parallel to the river and looking quite marooned, is a landing-stage (a simple raised platform no less than twelve feet by four, preferably fifteen feet by five or six) from the centre front of which a jetty (just a ramp) slopes down into the water. The landing stage still looks reasonably safe, but the jetty clearly is not. The effect could be heightened by three worn stanchions on each side, low at the downstage end of the ramp, knee height where the jetty joins the landing stage and hip height at the outside edge of the landing stage. There is a step to* CL *and one to* UL *of the landing-stage. To* R *of the landing stage is a very old bleached canvas seat and to* L *a couple of ancient wooden packing cases*

Finally, there is a clump of reeds and the odd bullrush at either end of the landing-stage to emphasize the overall effect, which is of a dilapidated and abandoned edifice, marooned on the water's edge and sinking slowly into the ooze from which it once arose. The bare cyc suggests a cold and cheerless day in late autumn. Strands of mist still cling to the reeds and jetty

The Fisherman — to all intents and purposes a harmless old man — is sitting perfectly still on his stool at the R *end of the landing stage or perhaps in a simple punt,* RC, *with his rod cast out into the water and a fishing basket beside him*

The Riverwoman, a distracted but resolute woman of sixty, mounts the step on to the landing stage from UL. *She doesn't see the Fisherman and he is reassuringly oblivious of her*

A sudden gust of wind chills her. A warning? She pulls her long cardigan closer about her, then steps forward again and comes, warily, down the jetty to the water's edge, where she stands waiting for the wood to adjust to her weight, gazing out across the water. Her head bows, but the memories still won't let her go. She leans forward and stretches out her hand, as close to the water's surface as she dare, but a strange fear has gripped her

Riverwoman (*to herself*) I must go!

A flock of geese flies noisily overhead

She backs up the jetty, tracing their journey through the sky, until she is once more on the safety of the landing stage. Her eyes take in the cold and empty skyline, upstage. She turns to look one last time at the water and, as she does so, she sees the Fisherman

(*To the Fisherman, bright but brittle*) I do envy them. Off on their winter holiday, lucky things.

Fisherman Who?

Riverwoman The geese. Back to Canada. Or the Arctic.

Fisherman They're not so daft. France. South of France now it's turned chilly.

Riverwoman But they're Canada geese!

Fisherman Might have been, hundreds of years ago. Now, they're like the rest of us. Want the easy life.

Riverwoman At least, when the time comes, they flap their wings and away. While I … Even in my dreams I'm here, still on the river bank, still …

Fisherman Stuck. I know the feeling. Right now, I've a raft of characters all caught on a sandbank, refusing to budge. So instead of "new day, new chapter", I write, "gone fishing" and land up here.

Riverwoman Can't you … give them a little … push?

He turns to face her for the first time

Fisherman Would it help?

She shakes her head

Riverwoman You're a writer!
Fisherman Sort of.
Riverwoman Fisherman?
Fisherman Sort of.
Riverwoman So we are both trapped at the water's edge, marooned on a landing stage, sinking back into primeval ooze.
Fisherman Funny that. Soon as people know you write, they start talking like novels.
Riverwoman Not a novelist …

He shakes his head. She relaxes

Philosopher?
Fisherman Huh!
Riverwoman I'm disturbing you.
Fisherman No. Only the fish.
Riverwoman Sorry.

Brief pause

I seem to remember, fishermen need silence. Silence and something…
Fisherman Fish need silence. Fishermen need patience.
Riverwoman That's it.

Brief pause

I really should be going. (*She sits*)

Fisherman (*indicating* UL) Am I right in thinking you own this place?

Riverwoman How can anyone own this … nowhere!

Fisherman But you own the land?

Riverwoman I do. Did.

Fisherman And so the water?

Riverwoman Water owns itself.

Fisherman Do you mind — my being here?

Riverwoman Ask the water.

Fisherman I did.

Riverwoman And what did the water say?

Fisherman To ask the Riverwoman.

Riverwoman (*fiercely*) "Riverwoman" now, is it? First they ring us. (*She points to her wedding ring*). "John's wife". Then they clip our wings with children. "Susanna's mother". But he's dead and she's long since flown the nest. Now, when it's my turn to take wing, they snare me with what I hate the most! "Riverwoman". Well, it won't work. This is my chance. My turn to fly!

Short pause

Fisherman Erm … is it all right for me to fish here … or not?

The Riverwoman turns and smiles at him

Riverwoman Stay. As long as you like. The place needs a man. Whenever I needed John, I knew where to find him: here, on guard. Said he was fishing. But I knew.

Fisherman You did need him, then?

She cannot face where this thought is leading and whips her mind on to something else. He listens as he throws out his line and settles down. He can wait

Riverwoman My husband built this. Not for fishing. Not then. For the boat. Used to go everywhere by boat in those days …

Or bike ... But most of the time we walked. People did in those days. Walk. Can't now, of course. Too far. Depend on others now. Penalty of age, dependence ... Where it all started. On the river. Me and a girlfriend. Our first holiday away from home, first time in the Fens. All so different then. Even this backwater flowed out to sea. And in the middle of the river, John, punting along. Looked so ... right, somehow. He waved, invited us aboard. Sylvia said, "Don't go near the water! Not safe down there". But I ... could see only the sun, flashing on the water ... not how deep it was. We came to this jetty — brand-new it was. He took my hand, walked me through the bullrushes, up the marsh meadow, across the fields — like no fields I'd ever seen. Most fertile in England, he said ... Didn't say they were never more than a whisker from flooding... On to his cottage, gleaming white like a lighthouse in acres of wheat. No one else around, no one for miles, just fields and ditches right down to the sea. But I looked up, not down, up into vast oceans of empty sky! And I could almost — almost — fly! I never went home again... Then winter came. And rain. Unending rain that swamped the fields, and drowned the roads, swilling and seeping its way into the kitchen. And all the time the sea boomed and clawed, boomed and clawed its way up the beach!

Fisherman If you didn't like it, why —— ?

Riverwoman Too late. I was pregnant. No escape when you're pregnant. And when Susanna came ...

Fisherman New life.

Riverwoman More like the end — of everything.

Fisherman You make him sound more like your jailer than your lover.

Riverwoman I loved him for freeing me from life at home; hated him for chaining me to this one.

Fisherman But you did need him...

Again she shrugs away this idea, refusing even to think about it

Riverwoman No-one belongs here, not this far out. It's land stolen from the sea and one day — one day quite soon now — the sea will reclaim its own.

Fisherman I remember when I first came here, all of this was under water. I remember flying low over the face of the water.

Riverwoman (*turning to him*) Alone?

Fisherman With my father.

Riverwoman What was it like here?

Fisherman Dark.

Riverwoman (*shivering*) Dark ...

Fisherman No light, no land, no people...Life only a dream, then ... Now it is yours.

Riverwoman And I have sold it— sold my inheritance for a mess of potage. Always wondered what that was, potage.

Fisherman Soup, I believe.

Riverwoman (*the fire building in her*) They say that's how life all began — in some primordial soup like this — creatures crawling from sea to swamp — hopping onto dry land — loping over grasslands — mounting the foothills. And why, Fisherman? When we stand on the pinnacle of the last and highest mountain — where's left for us to go but down — down across the dry land — back into the swamp — and out to open sea...

Fisherman Lady novelists!

Fisherman chuckles. She smiles. He rises

Riverwoman (*quickly*) Don't go! They said — you've got out of practice, that's all — with John dead and Susanna gone. Not right — lost out here in the marshes — with no-one but the bittern and the moorhen for company. One day — seemed even the birds were singing — Time to go ... On your way... Somewhere new. (*She smiles*) So I did. Found a cosy little flat — in the city. Lovely it is. Over a bakery — on a hill — what passes for a hill — dry land at least — cathedral, shops, a park — leisure centre, whatever that is — and people! So I've bought it. Know what decided me? The little shop bell going ping — ping all day long!

Fisherman Noisy.

Riverwoman Oh, but think of it! Ping! There are people, and ping! You're one of them, because ping! At last you are free! Free of this wasteland for —— (*She turns* L)

The Stranger, a volatile but vulnerable woman of forty, mounts the step from CL

The Riverwoman is startled, at first a little fearful of the younger woman

Stranger (*angrily*) Why didn't you tell me?
Riverwoman Hello, Stranger.
Stranger Is it any wonder when you never take me into your confidence?
Riverwoman (*defensively*) How could I? You were never here.
Stranger You could pick up the phone.
Riverwoman So could you.

Stalemate. Short pause

Stranger Thought I'd find you here.
Riverwoman Couldn't leave without saying good-bye.
Stranger To me?
Riverwoman To the river.

Short pause

Stranger Imagine how I felt, seeing the garden a mess, house empty. No sign. Nothing.
Riverwoman Much you care! You haven't been here since ...
Stranger I come every week.
Riverwoman Not to see me.
Stranger No.

Short pause

Riverwoman You timed it badly, then. Another few minutes, I'd have been out of your hair forever.

Stranger (*alarmed*) What d'you mean? Tell me!

Riverwoman Why should I?

Stranger I'm responsible.

Riverwoman You?

Stranger You need looking after.

Riverwoman I do not!

Stranger Yes, you do. You're old.

Riverwoman Not that old.

Stranger Must we have this discussion in public, Mother?

Fisherman Oh, don't mind me.

Stranger Who's he?

Riverwoman Himself.

Stranger He's no right here.

Fisherman I'm off.

Riverwoman Stay where you are.

Short pause

I haven't decided. I might stay here. (*She sits*)

Stranger Where? In the garden shed? With him? You need more than looking after. You need putting away. Oh, fetch your bags. You'll have to move in with me.

Riverwoman I will not!

Stranger I'm your daughter.

Riverwoman Not your child!

Stranger (*the pain showing through*) No. My child is ——

Riverwoman (*quickly, covering something neither of them can face*) I didn't want any fuss. I told the agent — Spring it was — no sign, no publicity. Just put it on your books.

Stranger He saw you coming. This place is a goldmine.

Riverwoman Gold?

Stranger With the right agent.

Riverwoman What would you know?

Stranger I read the adverts — go in, sometimes, take one of those sheets they do.

Riverwoman You've got a house.
Stranger Doesn't stop me dreaming.
Riverwoman Oh, dreaming!
Stranger A proper agent would've put it in the paper for a start. "Traditional three bed Fenland cottage".
Riverwoman Two.
Stranger Two and a box room.
Riverwoman It's not big enough for a box.
Stranger "Many original features".
Riverwoman And all of them damp.
Stranger "Large garden, riverside setting, own mooring".
Riverwoman I forgot that.
Stranger "A gem".
Riverwoman A wreck.
Stranger Says who?
Riverwoman The Estate Agent.
Stranger He would. Probably bought it cheap for himself.
Riverwoman That's just where you're wrong. Couple bought it straight off. And for the price I asked. Out-of-towners.
Stranger Strangers.
Riverwoman We're all strangers here … I'm just waiting to hand over the keys. Nice couple. Should be here soon. You'll meet them.
Stranger Thirties? Eager? Posh accent?
Riverwoman That's them.
Stranger They're here already. Man with them. Measuring.

The Riverwoman jumps up

Riverwoman They'll need to get inside.
Stranger They said no, outside's fine.
Riverwoman What's wrong with inside?

Stranger shrugs

I'm not ready for this! Not yet!

*For a moment, the Riverwoman struggles with her anxiety,
then off she rushes to see to them, exiting* UL

Stranger (*calling after her*) What about me? Driving past, seeing
  them. Slammed on the brakes. Raced up the path. Demanded
  what the hell they were doing. That's how I learnt you'd sold
  it! (*She stomps her foot in frustration*) Typical!

*Her action has frightened away the fish, so the Fisherman sighs,
stands up and reels in his line. She paces* L

She had no right to sell — no right at all!
Fisherman It was hers.
Stranger Should have been mine. My father ——
Fisherman Left it to her.
Stranger Not right.
Fisherman A proper little goldmine?
Stranger You think I give a damn about that? Or the house?
  It's here I ... Who are you, anyway? What're you doing here?
Fisherman I could ask you the same: why you still come here
  each week when you so clearly hate the place, hate your mother.
Stranger That's families for you. Can't stay together. Can't
  stay apart.
Fisherman So I gather.
Stranger Why? What's she said?

*She turns on him and approaches aggressively. The Fisherman
appears engrossed in baiting his line*

Fisherman What makes you so sure she ——
Stranger She's good at that. Getting people on her side. Even
  me, once. At my own daughter's funeral! She got the sympathy
  — I got the blame!
Fisherman Did they say that?
Stranger Didn't have to.
Fisherman Did the Coroner say that?

Stranger Accidental death. But they all knew. I knew… (*She turns and paces to the* UL *step*) What's she doing back there?
Fisherman You know. Showing them round. Where the fuse box is, meter cupboard, stop tap. The bathroom window that sticks in the rain. How to relight the old boiler that always blows out when the wind changes. Pointing out the hole in the kitchen drawer where your father dropped his hammer.

The Stranger turns upstage looking off, UL

Stranger She won't get away with — (*She stops and turns*) How come you …? (*Guessing*) You know David, my husband David.
Fisherman Not to speak to.

Geese fly over

Stranger (*distracted, off-guard*) All the same, you men. Think it's easy, letting go, moving on. Like those bloody geese. Autumn comes, you're off. Spring comes back, but he …
Fisherman You could have tried to find him.
Stranger Could have. Could have asked the neighbours. They'd know, some of them. But they were on his side, I could tell. Blamed me. Letting myself go. Clink of empty bottles in the bin.
Fisherman And were you — to blame?
Stranger You're from the Press! That's what you are — a bloody reporter!
Fisherman Writer.
Stranger Gutter press!
Fisherman No! I judge no-one. Observe and record, that's me.
Stranger (*sarcastically*) Every word and action?
Fisherman Every comma and full-stop.

Somehow this has backfired on her. She feels uncomfortable and returns to her restless pacing, heading L *this time. The Fisherman pays her no attention whatsoever. The chatter of moorhens*

Stranger What are you really doing here?

Fisherman Fishing?
Stranger You're not much good at it. (*She breaks away, but the
  fight has gone out of her*)
Fisherman Seems I can hook them; not quite reel them in. Not yet.

*She gives up, sits at the water's edge and slowly draws her knees
up to her chin*

Stranger I used to love it down here. My secret hideaway. From
  her. Dad knew. He was always here. We'd hear her calling,
  "Don't go near the water! Not safe down there". I'd giggle and
  he'd smile. In the summer, I'd swim in the shallows — it was
  safe then, I could see clear down to the riverbed ... safe, with
  Dad ... my own personal lifeguard. But he died. I couldn't
  come back, for must have been two, three years. Then one day,
  one hot summer day, I did. Only, there was a man, a stranger
  here, standing out in his boat in midstream, mapping the river
  bank. I stripped off, dropped my clothes in a pile and dived in.
  Why not? My secret place, not his! But he didn't see me. So I
  flipped on to my back and just lay there, with the sun flashing
  on the water — the weeds all around me — amazing how
  quick they'd grown. He saw me then. Waved. I pretended like
  I hadn't seen him, didn't care, who he was or wasn't. His job,
  he said, to keep the water safe. Check the culverts and ditches,
  keep the streams flowing to the river, the river out to the sea,
  stop the whole place ... drowning. And that was David. We
  met every day after that, till one day he said, fly away with
  me. I ran, fast as I could, up through the bullrushes, over the
  meadow, through the field, into the house; grabbed my bag;
  flew to the river ... and never went home again!
Fisherman Sounds like a happy ending. For you.
Stranger Autumn came; they moved him inland. And we moved
  to a house on that new estate. All right for him. He could escape.
  Each morning he'd drive off in the company car.
Fisherman Leaving you, stranded.
Stranger I was pregnant. Stuck indoors, with only a child for
  company! (*She rises*) What's your name?

Fisherman Cass.
Stranger Short for?
Fisherman Cassiel.
Stranger Not from round here, then.
Fisherman Nor are you, now.

The Riverwoman enters UL. *She approaches the jetty carefully,
a few flowers and grasses held carelessly in one hand*

*She calls out to them, but the Stranger cannot turn away from
the Fisherman's gaze. It is as though she has not really seen
him till now*

Riverwoman It's done. Nothing more to keep me here!

The Stranger turns away

Stranger Lucky you.

The Fisherman casts his line and settles down to wait

Riverwoman Lovely couple. She's pregnant. Did you notice?
  Soon be a new family here, new life.
Stranger They'll destroy everything!
Riverwoman Let them! It's dead already!
Stranger (*on a quick intake of breath*) No!
Riverwoman Such plans they have. Bring in the dredger, put
  an end to these weeds, re-open a channel to the river, so this
  foulness can wash clean out to sea …
Fisherman The fish will like that.
Stranger Not right!
Riverwoman If anyone's trespassing here now, it's us.
Stranger Please!

The Riverwoman hands the flowers to the Stranger

Riverwoman Visiting time's over. Time to say good-bye.

*They hold each other's gaze a moment, then the Stranger nods,
comes down the jetty, kneels and casts them on to the water.
Brief pause*

Fisherman What was her name? The little girl you lost?

The Stranger remains silent

Riverwoman Tell him.

The Stranger shakes her head violently

   You think he doesn't know? You think anyone doesn't know?
Stranger But he's a stranger!
Riverwoman Then let's make sure one stranger knows the truth!

Brief pause

Stranger Wendy. Her name was Wendy.
Riverwoman She was eight.
Stranger And a half.
Riverwoman It was half-term. So of course I had her.
Stranger I ... wasn't well.
Riverwoman I was baking ...Wendy was out in the garden.
   Doorbell rang. Tuesday afternoon, you see. Milkman. Have to
   pay the milkman. Then I made a cup of tea. Took the biscuits out
   of the oven. Called her. Went out, called again. Still no answer
   ... I started ... looking ... road, garden. Then searching. Fields,
   meadow ... Oh God, I thought, no! Finally — and I still don't
   know why — I came here. And there they were, in a pile, her
   clothes ... I phoned for help. You never answered.
Stranger I must have ... been asleep.
Riverwoman Tried David.
Stranger Should have been there.
Riverwoman (*mishearing*) I know I should! (*To the Fisherman*)
   They all blamed me! At the funeral — no-one said — all very
   kind — But I could tell — they were thinking ——

Stranger (*rising; quietly*) Me. They blamed me.

In a daze, she walks back up the jetty, while her mother explains

Riverwoman (*to the Fisherman*) At the inquest — they'd phoned me, you see, told me there'd have to be an inquest — the Coroner said as much. Accidental death. My fault, he meant.

The Stranger turns to her mother

Stranger (*genuinely puzzled*) No. Mine.
Riverwoman David said that, too.
Stranger My David? Blamed me?
Riverwoman Blamed himself. He wasn't on the river anymore to keep it safe; not at home for you. Too busy, too tired. Everything got left to you.
Stranger Not right.
Riverwoman That's what he said. It wasn't right.
Stranger He said all that? When?
Riverwoman He came round, at Christmas. Talked. All night he talked.
Stranger He never told me.
Riverwoman You never listened.
Fisherman So it was David's fault.
Riverwoman No.
Stranger Oh, never David's fault.
Riverwoman At least he loved her!
Stranger And you?
Riverwoman What about me?
Stranger You resented her!
Riverwoman I resented having her dumped on me whenever you'd had enough!
Stranger I … needed space. Wendy and I were close. That's what you resented.
Riverwoman And how long would that have lasted?
Stranger I loved her!

Riverwoman You loved David. Soon as Wendy came along you dumped him and loved her.

Fisherman How do you know that?

Riverwoman Because … because I know.

Fisherman (*firmly*) How, Elizabeth?

Riverwoman Because I felt the same. Only — only I got to hating your dad, blaming him for you, and you for keeping me tied down and her for never listening!

Stranger You? I thought ——

Fisherman So, who is to blame? That's what you want, isn't it — someone to blame?

Riverwoman Me.

Fisherman Susanna?

Stranger (*in a low voice*) No.

Fisherman (*lightly*) Then it must have been Wendy.

Riverwoman What possessed her? Time and again I warned her. Don't go near the water!

Stranger (*quietly*) Not safe down there.

Riverwoman When I found her little clothes, all piled up like that — just there they were. Whatever made her think it was safe to swim in … that!

The Stranger makes a strangled cry and moves away

Fisherman Susanna?

Stranger All right! It was my fault! There! I admit it! That's what you've all been waiting to hear, isn't it?

Fisherman Why?

Stranger Because I was drunk!

Fisherman Why?

Stranger I was always drunk!

Fisherman Why!

Stranger Because it was over! David, away all the time — then Wendy — already pestering to stay at her friend's — go on holiday with them. Leaving me!

Riverwoman Only natural. Growing up. Growing apart.

Stranger Didn't feel natural.

Fisherman And you were afraid.

Stranger How long before she too became a stranger?

Riverwoman She idolized you. Always asking: what you were like at her age. How would I know? Soon as you were old enough to be interesting, you were off out all the time. Where you going, I'd ask. "Nowhere." Who with? "No-one." Lord, you were difficult. Then you were gone. I had hoped — a daughter — we'd be friends.

Stranger I'd got friends.

Riverwoman So you said. Something else about that last holiday. She started quizzing me about your hideaway. Where was it? I told her, I'd be the last to know. It was always you and John, never you and me.

Stranger Oh, God!

Riverwoman Then she stopped asking. She'd come back for her biscuits — hair all wet, little dress sticking to her ——

Stranger She was only eight!

Riverwoman I asked her, What have you been up to? She gave me some nonsense about looking for the lifeguard!

For the Stranger this is too much. She makes a rush at the jetty to throw herself in

Susanna!

Suddenly there is the hollow sound of ancient timbers groaning and cracking as the jetty finally begins to give way. The Stranger is flung on to her back, terrified. She tries to scrabble backwards up to the safety of the landing stage

Stranger Mummy!

The Riverwoman sinks to her knees but cannot reach her

Riverwoman (*to the Stranger*) Take my hand. (*To the Fisherman*) Help me!

The Fisherman rises but does not move to help them

Don't leave me — not again!

The Stranger is sobbing freely now

Stranger I miss her, Mum.
Riverwoman So do I, love, so do I.

The Stranger turns to her mother, takes her arm and scrambles to safety. They hug

All right! So you were a rotten mother! So was I! So was my mother and her mother, right back to Eve. The woman hasn't lived who hasn't failed. All doing our best and all getting it wrong. The buck never stops till one of us takes our share of the blame, forgives herself and moves on.
Stranger (*shivering*) You're very wise all of a sudden.
Riverwoman Pity it's too late.
Stranger Is it?
Riverwoman Lord, I've just remembered. My mother said all this to me — forty, fifty years ago. If only I'd listened.
Fisherman Seems like not listening is something else that runs in families.
Riverwoman (*smiling, offering her hand*) I blame the parents.
Stranger (*smiling, taking her hand*) Most people do.

The Stranger starts juddering again. The Riverwoman strokes her hair

Riverwoman Over now, love. Over. Come on, allee -oop.

They help each other up

Fisherman Not Wendy's fault then.
Stranger No!

*The Riverwoman helps her to the old packing case where the
Stranger sits, her mother standing behind her*

Riverwoman Not hers. Ours. And we have to live with it every
day. I wasn't running away, love, only moving somewhere I
could see straight. (*To the Fisherman*) Maybe that's why we
need hills — hills and mountains — so we can look back and
make sense of how we got here. (*She sits*) Why David still
loves you I'll never know. But that's men for you.
Stranger David?
Riverwoman Talks about you all the time. Last time, just
yesterday, when he brought the van to help me move out.
He's waiting for me now, at the other end, to help me settle in.

*The Fisherman reels in his line. The Stranger rises and comes
forward to the water's edge*

Stranger Pity. The flowers don't move, just float on the surface.
No way through all these weeds to Wendy.

The Riverwoman joins her

Riverwoman Nothing we can do about that. But maybe it's still
not too late ... for us? To start again?
Stranger What as?
Riverwoman Mother and daughter?
Stranger Bit late for that. Friends?
Riverwoman Bit soon for that.
Stranger Then ... strangers? Hullo, I'm Susanna.
Riverwoman Elizabeth.

*The Stranger approaches with outstretched hand. The Riverwoman
rises. Their hands touch then quickly part. The Fisherman
unscrews his rod and begins to put his things away*

Fisherman Enough fishing for one day, I think.
Riverwoman But your writing?

Fisherman Even a comma in a story is progress.
Riverwoman Thank you.

From this point it is as if they cannot see or even recall him

Stranger (*to the Riverwoman*) Can I offer you a lift?
Riverwoman Yes. Then perhaps I can offer you a cup of tea.
Stranger If it's no trouble.
Riverwoman Oh, no. I'm sure David will have the kettle on, ready.

The Stranger draws back

   He'd love to see you.

The Stranger nods in agreement

Stranger Good-bye, Wendy.
Riverwoman Time to go.

If the Fisherman is in his punt, he picks up the pole and prepares for his journey. The two women make their way delicately across the marshy ground. Suddenly, the Stranger stops

Stranger That name. Cassiel. I keep feeling I should know it.
Riverwoman Only Cassiel I ever heard of was the Recording
   Angel.
Stranger Who?
Riverwoman You know, the one who writes down all we say,
   'all we do. Whatever made you think of him?
Stranger Oh!
Riverwoman What now?
Stranger There's water! Everywhere! My boots!
Riverwoman I keep telling you. It's rising. One day the sea will
   take it back. There'll be nothing but water as far as the eye...
   "And he flew over the face of the waters"... But surely!

Stranger
Wendy (*off*) } (*together*) Can we leave now?

The Stranger and the Riverwoman exit, arm in arm, UL

The Fisherman talks to Wendy as if she were there, but as with most conversations, he does not need to look at her, or make a pantomime of helping her aboard the punt. If he is on the jetty, he walks down on to the water and gathers up the flowers

Fisherman Yes, child. We can go home now.
Wendy (*off*) I thought they'd forgotten me. They never said my name.
Fisherman They were all choked up, like the water round here. Now, the river will flow and so will they.
Wendy (*off*) I thought they blamed me ...
Fisherman Should they have?
Wendy (*off*) I should have listened.
Fisherman They left you a present.
Wendy (*off*) Are those for me? They're lovely!
Fisherman Ready now?
Wendy (*off*) Ready.
Fisherman All aboard!

He walks towards UR *holding her hand, or he begins to punt them towards* UR

Wendy (*off*) Where to, Cassiel? Tell me again!
Fisherman Home, Wendy. Home.

Geese fly noisily overhead, the sound mingled with a child's happy laughter

CURTAIN

FURNITURE AND PROPERTY LIST

On stage: Landing stage and jetty
Two old packing cases L of the landing stage near back
Folding fisherman's chair
3-piece rod for coarse fishing set up
Weather-worn, open fishing basket with fishing
    paraphernalia (for **Fisherman**)
Punt (optional), with long rubber-tipped pole

Off stage: Few wild flowers and grasses (**Riverwoman**)

Personal: **Riverwoman**: wedding ring
Stranger: wedding ring

LIGHTING PLOT

To open: Late Autumn, exterior, morning, cold.

No cues

EFFECTS PLOT

Cue 1   To open   (Page 1)
Strands of mist clinging to the base of the reeds and landing stage; marshland bird cries

Cue 2   **Riverwoman:** "I must go!"   (Page 2)
Fade up Canada geese flying overhead, maintain for five seconds then fade under dialogue

Cue 3   **Fisherman:** "Not to speak to."   (Page 11)
Fade up Canada geese flying overhead, maintain for five seconds then fade under dialogue

Cue 4   The **Stranger** returns to her nervous pacing   (Page 11)
Moor hens chattering

Cue 5   **Riverwoman:** "Susanna!"   (Page 17)
Sound of splitting timbers as the jetty begins to collapse

Cue 6   The **Fisherman** moves down on to the water   (Page 21)
Strands of mist clinging to the base of the reeds and landing stage

Cue 7   **Fisherman:** "Home, Wendy. Home."   (Page 21)
Fade up Canada geese fly noisily overhead and a girl's happy laughter